Sunset Grand Couturier

Sunset Grand Couturier

Poems by

Myra Malkin

For Ellen—
with thanks for
your wonderful
poems and—even
on short acquaintance
—for your vividness.
Myra

Broadstone

Library of Congress Control Number 2021953458

ISBN 978-1-956782-01-1

Text & cover design by Larry W. Moore

Cover artwork, Tsukioka Yoshitoshi
Taira no Kiyomori (1118-81) stopping the descent of the sun c. 1876,
from the *Mirror of famous generals of Japan* series, 1876–82,
woodblock, 34.2 x 21.0 cm (image)
National Gallery of Victoria, Melbourne
Used by permission

Broadstone Books
An Imprint of
Broadstone Media LLC
418 Ann Street
Frankfort, KY 40601-1929
BroadstoneBooks.com

To my dear daughter and dear son-in-law,
Nadya Murray and Yoshi Kato

and in memory of Edward Murray

Contents

1. *THE POT-BELLIED I*

—James Ensor, *Mes écrits*

East West Home Best

He felt the loyalty we all feel to unhappiness—
the sense that that is where we really belong.
—Graham Greene, *The Heart of the Matter*

My would-be-quondam self, you shilly-shally
on the slummy side of the river. Stuck,

like the *citoyens* in Vuillard's drawing.
They line up at the Tuileries, to view
the opulent arcadia of others.

A tugging child.
A woman's close-clutched shawl,
her un-coiffed hair.

If I could choose to scrap
my first-draft self?
Glitter a little, be furred
with *amour-propre*?

—If I could *cross* that river,

could into color
stumble,
like Dorothy, from Kansas into Oz.

Would that be to betray
those ragged have-nots?
To disavow my unremodeled self?

—Yes. Better to bury wish, not stray.
Not blunder
into bloom.

Translated Cossacks

Suppose she happened to be descended
from a pariah-people, experts
at being scapegoats.

Cossacks came.
They burnt down the house.
All night, the family

crouched between the cornstalks.
Soot-flakes grazed them.
Relatives took them in—

they were *beholden.*
The mother kept nagging:
Let's go to America. Your uncle went.

Suppose the fear
got handed down
—like a tureen, a gene, a plated

pocket watch. In America,
they *still* were aliens.
Immitigable...

the sounds and signs
of Jewry that had burst
all bounds.

Sword-slashes they suffered:
the triumphs of peers; at weddings,
the condescension

of monied cousins; the
criticizing eyes
of the ensconced.

Her parents' wordless prompts:
be inconspicuous, be perfect,
be pretty, can't you

be pretty, damn it? She
was to certify them, be
laisser-passer for them. She was to make

a splash that would definitively scatter
the cousin-competition—but
modestly modestly. Ride

high—while lying low; lie
low—while riding high. No showiness
that might provoke

the evil eye; no gaffes, no boasts,
no overeager fervor—those footholds
for put-downs. But she lacked

the knack of it. Muzzled
her sumptuous *I am.*
Played safe; declawed herself.

It doesn't matter now.
New Cossacks are here,
new Kindly Ones:

old age;
marauding death.
Her *body* is an alien.

Shame Is the Shawl of Pink

—Emily Dickinson

The restaurant's very dark.
We order; I give her the shawl,
my gift from Japan.

Eagerly, she unshrouds it.
A sliver-pause
—like current going dead.

Then lukewarm thanks.
I see I've made a gaffe,
a gift faux pas.

I get a card. *In yesterday's dim light,*
the scarf looked grey. At home,
what stained-glass hues!

Maybe she really likes it—now.
Or maybe the card
is a lie. A fancier lie.

But I was right—
she didn't like it *then*. Sometimes they're twins:
the paranoid's assumptions and what's true.

Her judgment stung me—even if
a mis-seen scarf evoked it.
When I was five

my teacher-grandpa sat me down to take
what he called *IQ tests*—
to take my measure.

I overheard him say:
I thought that she'd do better.
—Deficient gift horse?

My outed self—
not fixable; a given.

Unwrapped, I disappoint.

Humiliation

Of all possible objects I was the most grotesque.
—Oscar Wilde, *De Profundis*

Like grief—
it won't degrade.

It's not
an early draft
that grace and labor
browbeat into flower.

It's not a detour
along the interstate to resurrection:
some day we will remember this, and smile.

It turns
the beleaguered ego
into that naked pin-up, Saint Sebastian.

It's cat piss
in the rugs of rented rooms,
an etched tattoo—

the pinpricked script
that all the perfumes of Arabia
are helpless to redact.

In the old coal-hole
of the self's
sub-basement,
the memory of it

squats.

A Voice Speaks of Othello, to Jealous Iago

The itch
of his magnificence!

He has *a daily beauty* in his life
that makes you ugly.

—That ease he has in having,
how it grates

on *him that ever fears he shall be poor*.
You plot. You deconstruct him.

You walk the unlit, muddy streets of Cyprus,
like Grendel, lured from sallow forest-closet

by clamor of mead-hall,
harp-hubbub, ruckus of revels—

the gloss that ill will *slubbers*.
—You want *Othello* slubbered.

You are not he. You never will be he.
Not ever ever ever to be he.

On flat black night—
the decals of the torch flames.

Mural from the Temple of Longing

—title of a painting by Paul Klee

It is the fireworks
that make me sad

—the tutu-selves,
the peacock-colored others.

Inside I am a rare Resplendent Quetzel,
but they are always playing not-my-music.

None of the doors
is higher than my knee.

I have no golden branch.
I have no key.

The Cup of Trembling

—Isaiah 51.17 and 51.22

I drive uphill.

To eastward,
where the dark is.

Gold gone.

Just fireflies left
—nomadic Yahrzeit glasses.

Milepost by milepost,
the thoroughfare
doles itself out.

That tacky vegetation by the roadside.
The soot-dark route,

the tarnish-colored blotches
of the tree-crowns.

Look at the segue of headlights
—those are the *good* children,
soon to be ironed by sleep.

No landscape now.

The leaky dark.
The monotone

of *I*.

Between the Lines

I do try.
I try not to be readable, I try not to be read.
I agree not to be read. I agree not to be real.
I pull the wool over everybody's eyes.
I pull a wool hat over my face, I taste
the saliva-y fuzz.

Because, in this country,
they shut words up in the Merriam-Webster Dictionary.
Exogamy
is not permitted.
Syntax
is not permitted.

Stay put, words. Hush, hush, words.
Stay unpronounced. Stay with your landsmen
in the ghetto of B, the remote province of Y.

—As if you could hide!
As if everything isn't a text that fizzes secrets.
I remember the basement, wall-to-wall in water,

that leakage of the true-blue sky.

A *Genji* Translator Visits an Exposition

At the Pavilion
of the Human Passions,

he ate *frites*
from a paper punnet.

He searched for what was covert.
On celadon saucers,
inaudible peonies' ghost-shapes.

He gazed at Altar-Calming Votive Objects.

I have understood, these last few days,
why old people kill themselves in spring.

—To feel life all around you and to feel
no life within.

Pathos of pottery fragments:
an ochre stoneware stack
of stuck-to-one-another serving dishes.

At least I have my Genji to go back to.
(I swear I will go back to it tomorrow.)

At the Pavilion
of the Human Passions,
a printed label listed Five Desires:

sex
food
reputation
property
sleep.

He looked for omens.
He asked the poem-cards
to tell his fortune:

The good
will not be solitary
long.

Brother-Animal

On Bleecker Street, a sidewalk selling-table.
A dune of handbags, drawstring pouches, wallets—
of zippered purses cut from carpet-fabric.

She's in a rush.
She's like a train, she eyes
what's just gone past—

nice fabrics—she's an addict
of containers.
She almost stops. She registers the sign.

And starts to cry.
—It's the spelling. The *mis*spelling.
Herself an expert speller,

a misspelled word affects her
as if it were the private body, published.
As if it were an injury, unbandaged.

A mirror of herself—or what she might be
if solid ground gave way.
(Of what she *will* be

when solid ground gives way.)
So undefended
against hope, this seller—

so hesitantly prideful,
this shortish, not-young man
behind his home-made sign.

I MAKE IT
ALL MYSELVE.

I Hate To Give Up Euphoria Altogether, So I'm Not a Good Buddhist

—Rudy Burckhardt

Along with feed bags, pitchforks, lawn-care products,
Agway sells statuary,
sells half-size Buddhas for the upstate garden.
"Buddha is very popular," says the salesman.

My name—almost an anagram of
maya. And of *Mara*—
she's the one who tempted Buddha,
underneath the sacred Fig, the Bo Tree.

Maya: illusion, world stuff—gotta love it!
On Eighty-Seventh Street
a lacquered Buddha leans against a tree trunk.
Lotus position. Chipped pink paint. *Sans* head.

Honeycomb

Terrain at the back of an 1850s farmhouse.

Irresolute breezes unravel.

The indolent muzzles of lilac
—they snuffle and bobble a little.

Sand, in a catalogue's sandbox,
moist
and lumpish in places.

Remnant of woods to the left, where, later,
your gerbil was buried.
Woods to the back,
where a skeletal car is upended.
Woods where—the seller apprised us—
a well is uncovered.

I—unaccustomedly peaceful.
You on the swing-set, in sandals,
out, after yesterday's rain.

Mama, you say.

Mama—
you're always the same.

I Love All Men Who Dive

—Herman Melville

Krasmanr:
to miss when throwing—

in one of the hundred-and-ten or so languages spoken
on aphoristic atolls,

in Vanuatu's
calico archipelago.

To throw's perchance to miss
—ay, there's the rub!

I heave atychiphobia to the wind
—old failure-fear, the scandal of disaster.

I recite the calligrapher's prayer,
the prayer at repeated embarkings:

O Lord,
do not make things difficult.

O Lord,
make everything come out well.

2. *STILL SO SAD, CONSTANZA?*

—from the libretto of Mozart's
Abduction from the Seraglio

A Trip We Took Before You Were Erased

Night on the Jersey Turnpike—
DETOUR notice.
No streetlights lit. *Route secondaire*. No signs.

Thick dark ahead—it roars at us like lava.
On either side, redacting night goes by.

Inside this darkness-larder—your blue shirt.
Your hands upon the steering wheel (bare wrists;
that décolletage of shirt-sleeves folded back).

The detour street decants us down its length
—past armed-guard trees—

as if some dead god dreams us,
as if we weren't sewn, now, to the earth.
No powers that be turn up, to readmit us.

To exits. Signage. Man-made clamor. Light.

Through the Looking Glass

Overnight,
I find myself enrolled

in the incredulous tribe—
the confraternity—

of those to jackal-habitat deported.

The death's door ones.
The diagnosed.
Their consorts.

My landsmen now.

I find I take some comfort in their numbers.
I cannot be a freak,
I'm one of many.

And yet—they frighten me,
these new companions.

Their tightened faces try to keep the secret
that candles burn on altars to no purpose.

That no enactment bars these natural murders.

That gods from the machine
—like bureaucrats or plumbers—

are overworked,
and deaf to rage or prayer.

Near the Hospital

1
Sun paints her with itself,
it drowns out grief.

If only she could lie down on the sidewalk,
if she could rest her head

against the mica-glitter.

Strangers would come.
They'd lift her.

They'd put her somewhere
that was not her life.

2
She makes her way
to Fifty-ninth,
up Tenth. Past taco shops.

She climbs uphill,
a slope once dense with brush,
with thick-trunked trees.

Here—underneath
the unkempt jungle-gym
of steam pipes, mains—

is ancient earth,
old tight-packed soil,
old earthworm-threaded dark.

Then bedrock's
adamantine stop
—kind terminus.

Touch and Go

The daylight came and went.
You came and went.

I am inquorate now.
Outline lacking—
Chinese *boneless painting*.

You are just a pulse now, not a presence.
You are the scotoma

—like a black-spot spider,
up against the brightness.

At the wedding breakfast
—under siege by sunlight—
butter pats were melting.

Now the blue-black evening.
Now the salt flat, absence.

Japanese Lesson

Shinda hazu no hito, doshite koko ni iru n' desu ka?
—Japanese language textbook

The person who is supposed to be
dead—
why is he here?

The person who is supposed to be
here—
why is he dead?

Spring air
—so promise-crammed. He used to say
it should be bottled.

O bottled past, from which
saved photos shut me out.

Broken, forever,
the red strings of his zither.

A Cloud on Title

An outstanding claim or encumbrance which, if valid,
would affect or impair the title of the owner.
—Black's Law Dictionary

For 21 months: full black
(a large Mourning Department
at Marshall & Snelgrove's).
Segue to grey—lilac and lace, with pearls.

In the hospital lounge,
a redhead, on her cell phone:
"It's twelve years, but I keep my wig.
He saw me without my boob,
but never without my *hair*, not ever *bald*."

ULLAGE:
the amount by which a container
fails to be full of liquid.

Winnicott's patient says, "Today,
I won't reach
for the travel rug.

Because I want
Something That Will Not GO AWAY.

—What never goes away's the *not*.

So all I have
is what I have not got—

no rug
is what is real."

No rug's
the iceberg—not the ship.
(We'd rather have the ship,
the boob,
the rug.)

An insufficiency
of DUNNAGE:
loose packing stuff, stored among casks, to prevent
chafing, or breakage.

(Let Joanna contend with the anchovy,
for FRICTION is inevitable.)

A breach
in the Maginot Line, a cloud
upon title:

the penciling of that dreadful It
by which we finally will be hit.

A smaller net loss
than expected?

A *total* loss.

The iceberg
DWARFS
the ship.

Expelled from Furnished Eden

Right away the trucks came—
Juggernaut Content Liquidators came.

What's left?
Before's bequest.

Dry lake.
A concrete steppe. Exile in place.

These dandelion ghosts
—no matrix-grass,

no outsized sky, the stew from which the stars
insist, insist.

No syntax hasps.
The orphaned objects parody still lifes:

a roll of strapping tape,
a widowed shoe.

Who killed
my gilded geese?

Now just these planters—trash cans—
what is left

after the trucks have left.
No sugar castles left. I'm left.

—So decorous.
Here I and sorrows sit.

Wallis-Wallace

How many women have covered themselves with dew. . . .
—Wallace Stevens, *The Man on the Dump*

At the inn owned by Mr. and Mrs. Zucotti,
you got into bed with a coffee-table book.
A whole book about Wallis Simpson's jewelry.

You weren't very interested in jewelry,
but you were a minutiae-collector—
you liked fact-baubles.
Anything you read,
you remembered it forever.

The dump
is full of images.

Mrs. Zucotti's husband had been the maître d'
at El Morocco.
And the Occupy Wall Street park was named for her son.

You couldn't know about the son.
—When you were in elementary school, you told me,
you got a star
for Current Events.

Where you are now, though,
there aren't any current events.
No *there* there.
Although, when I picture the dead,
they're sitting around an old TV
in the monotonous nursing home of heaven.

Finnegan woke, but Finnegan broke.
Finnegan croaked.
Erotic defense
dooms Jets.

How ugly that jewelry was.
The diamond and onyx panther,
the *crystal tableau.*
Dump-glitter. Ruin's armor. Stones,
her stanzas.

I remember it forever
—you, in your broadcloth pajamas,
reading me lists of the Duchess of Windsor's adornments.

A Pang Is More Conspicuous in Spring

—Emily Dickinson

The dither of this whiteness,
this petal-assemblage
—I can't absorb it.

Each year, a white allée:
these Callery Pears, in bloom on West Eleventh.
Each year I want to show them to the dead.

—But would those dead remember who I am?
By now they may be vague
about our once-shared past,

may be serenely lost
in Paradise, that lavish athenaeum,
the domed round reading room of Kingdom Come.

In that unhurried *always* of the dead,
each porous self's a textile of antennae.
Time's stretchy, like sea-taffy—

all day the dead can dally
amid *is*, *was*, and *will be*,
those crowded, simultaneous bazaars.

This modest here-and-now?
A small beclouded patch upon that canvas
—my face, my tears,

these ferris wheels of white.

Too Many Waltzes Have Ended

—Wallace Stevens

Only a stone's throw away—
my youthful, acquisitive self,
amassing housewares at Macy's basement or Zabar's.

Exchanging wedding presents, impulse buying:
cutting boards, roasting pans,
canisters, pepper mills, muffin tins.

I still have
the stainless steel dish
Miss Elo gave us.

My father's secretary—Elo, she liked to be called.
Plump-cheeked, theater-going, gallantly unmarried,
she lived on Perry Street in Greenwich Village.

When my mother got sick,
Elo sent knobbly branches, floweret-stippled.
And just a few years later she too died.

It's dishwasher-safe,
her wedding-present cookware.
I'd put it in the broiler—

make melted cheese with Worcestershire, on toast.
I kept it when I moved
—a widow-platter.

Disappearing Act

It still is blue,
the swath I see of sky.

If you were here,
we'd walk a few more blocks

—like day,
we'd be reluctant to decamp.

Off to the west,
a pink embankment drifts

—cloud-skeins
the river's mirror discomposes.

And upright lakes of light—
tall windows that reflect

the azure tracts
of still un-sated day.

Low house fronts, though, are dark,
as if they served as savings banks for harm.

Soon stockpiled dusk
will cuttlefish the air

—the monologue of night
will blot out all.

Fifty-Eighth Street

Fifteen years have passed

and I still don't like
to be on 58th Street.
To walk along the flank
of the hospital.

You were at that hospital,
when a patient jumped
out of a ninth-floor window.
Police came;
they cordoned off the street.

Further east,
there's still a jewelry store.
A shoemaker, a laundromat,
a nail salon.
—What a homey street.

What would it be like
to arrive in the afterworld,
and be apprised
that no more suffering
would be inflicted?

No dispossessions.
No flesh-humiliations.

For how long
would memory

still burn?

Spooky Action at a Distance

—Einstein's description of quantum entanglement

The physicist's pair:
two parted particles.

Although they do not touch,
they are—a term of art—

entangled. Just like us.
We too can now

not touch
—*entangled* in now's *less*.

The *less* that is so scant,
the *less* that's so much less

(to *fixe* from *explosante*)
than what the past vouchsafed.

Speak to me
—my complementary one.

Speak oxymorons to me.

3. *SCREAMING ABDABS*

Little Dada Night Lied

That conscious piece of you
at three a.m., that modest

Alp
of you.

The underwater bulk that is
the rest of you,

the loosened glue, the furry
rest of you.

Vainly, you seek
the unpropitious hinterlands of sleep.

You are a ghost,
the ghost

of a blancmange.

Dread

Monochrome of night-time.
Bleecker Street is noisy:

sidewalk tables; beer steins;
light from plate-glass windows.

Every self's a furnace.
Each a thrum that, separate,

pollinates the darkness.
Night's a dream I'm dreaming,

panicked by my transience.
I'm the stateless dreamer,

outside night's enclosure.
—An armistice with fate

has come undone.

Wet

We'd brought my father home (a trip upstate).
Some child above had left a faucet on:
one bedroom wall a drizzling waterfall;
framed pictures—backings soaked.

He had no head for chaos left. He howled.

And once I seemed to wake,
my own house full of rain.

Wet house,
found myself in, my onetime
house, blebbed walls, my
roofless house—
wet carpet underfoot,
my staircase wet.

How long before I knew it to be dream?
Woke. To no drench. No floods.

Weather Advisory, 10/28/2012

There are handkerchief ghosts in the playground
and row house stoops festooned

with taffy-pulls of cotton.
And lipsticked little girls wear sequined dresses.

It's unseasonably warm.
Couples are drinking wine at outside tables—

waiters in rolled-up sleeves, in natty aprons.
It's like a photograph;

the trees still have green plumage.
How can they say a hurricane's approaching

—it's as if you had a disease
but—not yet—any symptoms.

Despoliation's coming.
If only it could be

the haiku's one-note frog-splash.

Which interrupts
a stillness

—but ratifies that stillness.

Public Health Dream

I dreamt of baobabs.
(They call them upside-down trees.)

Then the haboob came, a desert dust storm.
Walls of sediment rammed me.
The sand seemed to guzzle up the air.

I dreamt that scurvy politicians
—slivers of ice in their hearts—
stood on a hillock of mud.

They were washing their hands.

Lies sallied forth from them,
as excrement
and semen.
Fibs, half-truths, porkies, alternative facts.
A sewage haboob.

I hid myself in scutch grass.

Meanwhile, the dead piled up.
I mean the unrefrigerated dead.
People of so-called color.
Bus drivers—orderlies—firemen.
Food service workers.

The air was like minestrone.
Lies filled it. Lies
in their aerosol go-carts.

The baobabs died.

—What happened afterward,
I can't remember.
I drifted away
to the empty suburbs of sleep.

SARAH CHARLESWORTH'S FALLING BODIES

Each photo shows a body
—a single body, falling from a building.

Cropped
newspaper photos.
Re-photographed. Enlarged.
Six-and-a-half feet tall.

In Siskind's photos of divers
—*The Pleasures of Levitation,*
The Terrors of Levitation—
an unframed void: whiteness
that must be sky.

Charlesworth's figures are drowning
in greyish pixels.

Low-res. Ric-rac.
Graininess, fuzziness, blur
—memory's batty redactions,
the antechamber of waking.

People say a fall feels
longer
than its stopwatch measure.

One woman's nightgown
seems to be riding up.

A critic writes:
maybe she jumped,
maybe there was a fire.

What is enlarged
is terror—

the door to the dark,
ajar.

Nature Is Too Green and Poorly Lit

— François Boucher

Ravel: Does it not occur to people
that I may be artificial

by nature?

—His father invented
a somersaulting car.

Hans Hofmann to Jackson Pollock:
do you work from nature?

I *am* nature, said Pollock.

And Galway Kinnell wrote:
Whatever / what is is

is what / I want.
(He wanted a trio: is,
three times in a row.)

It makes grammatical sense.
But given the errant nature of *what is*,
does it make sense to *want* it?

—Nature: whatever is?

In a story by Isaac Singer,
a man named Meyer
—I was named
for some great-uncle Meyer—
argues that there is no such thing as *error.*

All things that are
are hatched by the Divine.
How can there, then, be error?

There is a chrysalis in which
base-metal-error's sea-changed into gold.

Is body-pain transformed? Pain
is an error.

Those palliative spheres
are not *what is.*

Breakable Perishable Hazardous Liquid

End of the pier.
The wind-flicked water pleats my liquid shadow.

Swan Lake last night.
And yesterday the tests—

the fortune-telling, see-through-flesh machines.
Last night I lost my necklace, lapis

lazuli—loose catch. It slipped from me.
Grief for a necklace? Even while I fear

a complot of my cells? *Swan Lake* last night—
misfortunate Odette.

Beyond my shaky river-self, I see
a grid of pilings, where an old pier lay.

—Let me not be
among those turned forever into swans.

Mine Enemy Is Growing Old

—Emily Dickinson

Resentment starts to falter.

Now it is getting harder
to safeguard hoarded anger.

One rival's in a wheelchair.
One foe, dementia's kidnapped.

How much do I still feel?
I don't know how to measure

this threadbare, antique rancor.
It's like old currency that can't be spent—

outmoded francs, anachronistic lire.

Old Woman, Walking in the City

Too swiss-cheese a terrain.

Alcoves of absence
—like niches without their colossi.

And every year, more sites to turn away from.

The four-block hospital compound.
A restaurant, at lunch time—

the friend who never got there
(being, by that time, dead).

Like hot spots on a PET-scan,
where sweet-toothed cancer snuffled up
investigative sugar.

The self's own cancellation, just ahead.

Notice of Discontinuance of Benefits

Your roommate body—
for years, she partied with you.

Suddenly, she's sick. She needs new parts.
Needs scans, needs EKGs.

You're good to her—you go to doctors with her,
you sit with her at night.

She's angry, though. She says you colonized her.
You were the governor-general

who trafficked in slaves,
who squandered her bauxite, her gold.

And now the indigenes
rebel, they besiege the capital.

They dismantle
the collaborative city.

Mulberry, Shade Me, Shade me a While

—Wallace Stevens

I am Cyrus,
king of the universe,
king of Babylon, king of Sumer and Akkad.
May Marduk, the great lord,
grant me a long life!

—Who does not say this?

A textile display:
the socks of a Carmelite nun.
Apart from their mended lacunae
they hardly exist.
They want to go *on* being socks,
as I—almost equally darned—
would like to go on being *me*.

Save the Whales. Save Water. Save the Earth.
—No, no, no, save *me*.

Save *me*, Marduk.

Let me be a regular
at the Never-Fade-Away Café.

Do not truncate my act.
Do not dispatch the vaudeville hook
to yank me from the stage.

When fear un-shells me,
hear me.
Hear me, Marduk.

Complaint of the Amorous Dead One

Dead now.

Dry-curing—like a hung ham
(on my way to becoming a spirit
as perfect as bacon)—

bodiless, almost,
in this lugubrious gondola, this coffin.

I dally,
a bus queue of one—
still mourning for my paramour, the world.

—Ex-paramour, alas. The world disdains me.

Haven't you heard of the hat, the invisible hat,
that cancels out the damsel who thinks to sport it?

My milliner, Death, bestowed it.

The green hills are brown now
in Piero della Francesca's
St. Jerome and a Supplicant.
—That's what happens
to copper resinate pigment.

Vanish like hailstones! Go!
All flesh is grass.

Solipsist

Hurricanes, famines,
suicide bombers.

Their victims—the extinguished—
all whom the flood did, and fire shall o'erthrow.

I lie in the dark, afraid
for footholdless have-nots.
For sea-threatened continent-islands.

But really thinking only of myself.

Monotonously wanting
more time,
no pain,
no pain,
more time.

As if I weren't merely
a fungible iota,
as if I weren't kin
to the ant, the mite, the krill.

As if I were,
instead,
a whole endangered species

—one that ought to be *listed*
by the Fish & Wildlife Service of the Department
of the Interior—

on whose behalf,
nature conservancies
ought to be suing

Nature.

Nothing of Us But Doth Fade

The Remote Annunciator
—the Central Warning Panel—
is silent now.

Its lights are out.
There's nothing to transmit.
Like everything else, the Remote

Annunciator
—and other apparatuses and baubles—
are underneath the planet's Alpine waters.

Slime bejewels them.
Waffle irons, vacuum cleaners, popcorn makers.
Cell phones, declawed of ringtone.

The washing machines
are full but just with water.
Their porthole-doors flap open

with only a putative sound
—like the vertical trees
when, wind-uprooted, they toppled

(no one to hear their landings,
their branch-dismembering
nose dives).

In dirty-windows water,
the teeth of the ocean are working,
to undo objects' outlines.

Rotted sequoias subside
onto the yard sale seafloor

—where all our insubstantial pageants lie.

4. *ALL THE BLACK SAME I DANCE MY BLUE HEAD OFF!*

—John Berryman, *Delusions, Etc.*
("King David Dances")

The Fox Know Many Things, The Hedgehog Only One

—Archilochus

A jack-of-all-trades fox is what I am,
but what I long to be

is hell-bent hedgehog, one-track-minded workhorse
—a Turner, indefatigably scumbling,

a woodblock-making *old man mad on drawing.*
Not I; I am a fox—an omnivore,

restless, digressive, detour-tempted, greedy,
a print-addicted, whale-throat entryway

for ocean flotsam—scraps, which I immure
in notebook-urns, in shoebox ossuaries.

An ant with outsize crumb—
my data-hoard, my archive of obsession

—which needs a making-small machine, to store it,
an engine that condenses—something like

that reMARKable work,
The Bible, in Pitman Shorthand.

—No, no, I'm off again.
I want to be possessed by just *one* want:

to be a glass-hard node—by crystal stickpins stabbed—
a hedgehog-chandelier, a fizgig's transfixed flare—

a fistful of soliloquizing light.

I Want I Want for Ever and Ever

—John Arden, *The Happy Haven*

Before she goes to sleep,
I read a bedtime story to my daughter.

I have to read it twice or even three times—
each sameness like a promise that's unbroken.

It's as if she already senses
that time will repossess

the child's carte blanche, her cornucopias.
But now, in her sleepy palace,

she has it in her power
to make the present last—and last—and last.

Read it again, she says
—imperious daughter!

Read it again!

Is't Not Fine to Dance and Sing, While the Bells of Death Do Ring?

—Elizabethan song

When they assault my eyesight
—the thick, black, waxy petals
of these tulips—

that plague, mortality,
is in remission.

And when I taste
chorizo
con chocolate

—thin thumb-shaped sausage slices;
a slathered
salt-sweet spread—

then grief
and limbo-terror
go away.

There's no one here but Self—
the Hungerer.

And the dead,
with their memory-switchblades,
go wait by the door
—there's too much *now* for them:

these body-hubbubs,
these short-lived scalding
sunsets
of the senses.

Baudelaire's Mistress, Painted by Manet

Across the horizontal canvas-steppe,
her gauze skirt's splayed—
a palimpsestic waterfall of white.

Her little skinny stockinged
shin sticks out.
Her fan's a greenish black, her pretty slipper's

black. And like a little porthole into night:
her postage-stamp-sized face
—her shoe-black stare.

It's Baudelaire's *perfect monster,*
his *old cauldron,*
it's the *wayward and dolorous Creole,* Jeanne Duval.

The brothel-worker's daughter *kicked my cat out,*
never thanks me,
DOESN'T ADMIRE ME.

Like waves harassing shore,
he keeps addressing her
—his *nymphe macabre.*

You're not fresh anymore—
no, my very dear.
You have the shininess

of too much use.
But you are still—to me—still séduisante.

The Handbag Inspector, at 3:00 A.M.

He dreams
he is on horseback; he reviews

black handbag maws,
those secret-keeping crows.

—Here is his wand, his punctilious torch.
Its mouth is a delicate grommet:

it sniffs at the lipsticks, the tickets,
it palpates the cul-de-sac alcoves.

Now he is swimming, in night-silk.
He floats in the musky seraglio,

he loses himself in the grottoes.
Now he is pouched, he is shrouded.

Now he is zippered. He sleeps.

Ida Haendel

She never married.

Her father
—and not only he—
thought of her as an instrument.
As co-extensive with her violin.

Somebody asked her why she let that happen.
Why sacrifice her private life for music?

Nobody ever came to me and told me:
Put down your violin, we're getting married.

Perhaps she was waiting.
—Then she got bored with waiting.

Some diner, biker-filled, at one a.m.
She and a cellist colleague
talk about Schumann—
his D-minor sonata, for piano
and violin.

The cellist: *I hardly know it.*

She played it for him—him and all the bikers.
A storm of applause at the end
—clapping and hooting and stomping.
Aural bouquets.

A fresh cup of coffee for Ida Haendel!

Mere Freaks of Chromomania

—a critic's comment, at Turner's 1840 Royal Academy exhibition

Wet-into-wet.
So *emulous of light.*
Paint-arsonist—*yon angry setting sun.*

The weave of canvas surfaces, paint's crusts
—to feel them with my tongue!

Black sails, black ships, a *Burial at Sea*
—the sails *too black* for Ruskin. Turner says:
if I could make them blacker still—I would.

Storm-paroxysms, fire-at-sea carousals.
Painter and Nature: chaos-virtuosi.

Hope, Hope! fallacious hope!
Lost to all hope, the brig. . . .

His vortices.
His muted
sea-sky sutures.

His Roman-candle-like transliterations
of fickle, insurrectionary light.

Drummer, Tuning

The timpanist,
that adept of hiatuses,

with cashmere taps
begets
mute booms, like ghosts.

He has to tune—fine-tune—
his hubbub-kettles
—the stew-meat timbres in them.

Soft auguries
of flams,
of pataflafla-gabble, plush tattoos.

He lays his cheek
against the taut-drawn skin,

as though the endless rests
—while violins and trumpets perorate—
have magicked him to sleep.

But his attentive ear
still hearkens
to his heavy creatures—hears,

as if it were in escrow, their intent.

Their pent-up spate,
their reservoirs of roar.

I Dream of an Imaginary Mirror

A mirror's propped
beside the satin lap
of Mary Magdalene.

Upon that lap, at ease,
a chubby baby lies.

The mirror frames the polyhedral folds
of white and purple silks, and elbow-flesh

—mute landscape, into which
a sleepy child might press

blind open mouth,
a hide-and-seeking face.

Like the flaw that the maker leaves
(to tempt ill-luck to exit)
in the crimson and dead-leaf beige

of an opulent carpet's
arbor of half-palmettes,

this brush-stroked mirror serves
as aperture: a doorway into rest,

an Eden-swatch,
a square of abstract pattern, among stuffs.

Inside it, nothing but
silk syllabub of touch.

Pellucid sleep.
Skin's heat.
Clouds' color-flush.

Reading MacNeice

Dissolved in the running water of time, we fool our fancy
To catch intact what is always in dispersal.
— Louis MacNeice, "Departure Platform"

Haven't read through the *Collected Poems*,
but even if I had,
if I had pencil-marked
lines I especially liked—

world is crazier and more of it than we think—

would I remember those lines?
One poet, one *Collected Poems*, one life.
So much to know about him, to forget.
When his mother died, he was five.
He started writing poetry at seven.

The party he spent by a mantelpiece—elegant, silent.
His host said:
Is it true you were brought up in Belfast, at Carrickfergus?
—Yes.
Ah, that confirms a legend I have heard:
a long time ago, seals invaded that coast
and interbred with the folk there.

Even when I copy whole poems
into my current notebook,
some of them slide from my head,
like keys from an unzipped purse.

I go on doing it, though.
Those hospitable notebooks,
—those cabinets of curiosities
It's like somebody taking selfies:
Buckingham Palace and me,
Louis MacNeice and me.

Why this compulsion to cull,
to salvage sea-glass fragments?

As if I'm stuffing loot
into a too-small sack,
and running from a wreck
—though it's I who am going to sink,
and all too soon.

As I am drowning,
I'll wave
—as well as I can—

my darlings clutched to my chest.

Conversation Piece

Lady Throckmorton (Bess)
—Sir Walter Raleigh's wife.

(*Queen Bess* was Bette Davis;
Joan Collins played plain Bess.)

King James had Raleigh beheaded.
Sir Walter at the block cried *Strike, man, strike!*

Set on my soul an everlasting head.
—Thus ended his *short light.*

Some underling embalmed the severed head.
Bess took it home, and everywhere she went

—like Mary with her lamb—the head went too.
(For one addicted to continuance,

no more incongruous than death itself,
or plastic-coffered characterless ash.)

What did Bess store it in?
A Jacobean haversack perhaps?

—A scarlet leather pouch, says one account.
Had she a minion whose task

was to carry that sack?
In the flurry of some departure,

did a frazzled servitor shout:
Who has the head?

Notes

Sunset Grand Couturier: from Ezra Pound's *Cantos* (the last line of Canto 80).

"East West Home Best": The Tuileries is a public garden in Paris, near the Louvre.

"Translated Cossacks": *Immitigable. . . bounds*—from *The American Scene* by Henry James.

"Humiliation": *Some day we will remember this and smile*—from Virgil's *Aeneid*, I.203.

"A Voice Speaks of Othello": *a daily beauty*—in the play, Iago says this of Cassio, not of Othello. Grendel is one of the monsters in *Beowulf*.

Mural from the Temple of Longing: The Resplendent Quetzel is the national bird of Guatemala. The composer Igor Stravinsky is supposed to have said, on some occasion, "Why are they playing not my music?"

The Cup of Trembling: A Yahrzeit glass is a small container for a Yahrzeit candle. Some Jews light such candles on the night before the anniversary of a death, and keep them lit for 24 hours.

"A Genji Translator": Except for the last stanza (for which I haven't found a source), the quotations are adapted from Edward Seidensticker's *Genji Days*.

"Touch and Go": A scotoma is a blind spot in an otherwise more or less normal visual field.

"A Cloud on Title": Marshall & Snelgrove was a London department store, Donald Winnicott an English psychoanalyst and writer. The lines about the iceberg allude to Elizabeth Bishop's "The Imaginary Iceberg" ("We'd rather have the iceberg than the ship"). *The penciling of that dreadful it*—inscribed by Stephen Spender in one of Lucian Freud's sketchbooks. *Let Joanna*—from Christopher Smart's "Jubilate Agno." The Maginot Line, a series of defensive fortifications in France, was constructed in the 1930s as a barrier to German invasion.

"Expelled from Furnished Eden": *Here I and sorrows sit*—from Shakespeare's *King John*, III, 1, 73.

"Spooky Action at a Distance": *fixe. . . explosante* is borrowed from the title of a piece (*explosante—fixe*) by the composer Pierre Boulez.

"Public Health Dream": A haboob (hab-OOB) is a violent dust storm.

"Sarah Charlesworth": Charlesworth and Aaron Siskind were American photographers.

"Old Woman": A PET-scan is a medical imaging device. It uses a tracer, a radioactive sugar, that shows up in areas of the body that may be diseased.

Mulberry, Shade Me: Cyrus II (Cyrus the Great) was the king of Persia in the sixth century B.C. and the conqueror of Babylon. Marduk was the patron god of Babylon.

"Complaint of the Amorous Dead One": *St. Jerome and a Supplicant*, c.1460-64, by Piero della Francesca, is in the Metropolitan Museum of Art. *Vanish like hailstones*—from Shakespeare's *The Merry Wives of Windsor*, I, 3, 81.

"Solipsist": *all whom the flood did*—from "At the round earth's imagined corners," a sonnet by John Donne.

"Nothing of Us But Doth Fade": A remote annunciator is a central control panel, which displays the status of the equipment or the systems in a building, aircraft, etc. *Insubstantial pageants*— adapted from Shakespeare's *The Tempest*, IV,1, 155.

The Fox Knows Many Things: The Japanese painter Hokusai described himself as *an old man mad on drawing*. A fizgig is a hissing firework.

"Baudelaire's Mistress": Jeanne Duval's portrait (1862) is in Budapest's Museum of Fine Arts; *wayward and dolorous Creole* is from Felix Fenéon's comments on the painting. The 5th stanza complaints are adapted from Baudelaire's letter to his mother, 27 March 1852. *Perfect monster, old cauldron*, and the last two stanzas are paraphrases of lines in Baudelaire's "Le Monstre."

"The Handbag Inspector": In New York City, guards are often posted at the entrances to museums and concert halls, to inspect visitors' bags.

"Ida Haendel": Haendel (1928-2020) was a Polish-born violinist, who started out as a child prodigy. The diner story is from her obituary in the *New York Times*, 7/8/20.

Mere Freaks of Chromomania: J. M. W. Turner (1775-1851) was an English painter; *emulous of light, yon angry setting sun*, and *Hope, Hope* are from his poem "Fallacies of Hope." *If I could make them blacker still* paraphrases Turner's response to John Ruskin, the Victorian art critic.

"Drummer, Tuning": Flams and pataflaflas are basic drumming patterns; a tattoo is a kind of military music.

"I Dream of An Imaginary Mirror": The painting in the dream is based on *Martha Reproving Her Sister Mary*,1620, by Orazio Gentileschi, Alte Pinakothek, Munich. (There is no baby in the painting.) Mary, the sister of Martha, is sometimes identified with Mary Magdalene.

"Reading MacNeice": *world is crazier and more of it than we think*—from "Snow," a poem by Louis MacNeice. The seals anecdote paraphrases a passage in *Six Poets: Hardy to Larkin*, edited by Alan Bennett. (Bennett says he heard the story from Stephen Spender.)

"Conversation Piece": *Strike, man, strike*—Raleigh is supposed to have said this to his executioner. *Set on my soul an everlasting head*—from Raleigh's poem "The Passionate Man's Pilgrimage"; *short light*—from Raleigh's "Lines from Catullus."

Acknowledgments

Grateful acknowledgment is made to the following publications in which these poems have previously appeared:

"Expelled from Furnished Eden"—*Fading Light* (anthology), Taylor & O'Neil

"Wallis-Wallace"—*Mudfish* 19

My warm thanks to former teachers Deborah Landau, Dennis Nurkse, and Martha Rhodes. Thanks, yet again, to Susana Case, Elizabeth Haukaas, Laurence Loeb, and Lynn McGee, for advice, encouragement, active nudging, and useful criticism, and thanks to Stephen Frankel for help with finding a cover. I am very grateful to Larry Moore for welcoming me to Broadstone Books, and for his kindness, his patience, and his dry sense of humor. Many thanks to all the friends who sustain me with conversation, memory-grazing, wry laughter, shared rage, commiseration, quotations, lavish emails, grammar discussions, and love. Finally, since I feel with Frank O'Hara that "I can't even enjoy a blade of grass unless I know there's a subway handy," a grateful salute to my once-again home, New York City.

About the Author

Myra Malkin is the author of *No Lifeguard on Duty* (Mainstreet Rag Publishing Company, 2010). In 2016, in a contest judged by Edward Hirsch, her poem "Wallis-Wallace" won the 12th Mudfish Poetry Prize. After growing up in New York City, she studied acting at the Royal Academy of Dramatic Art, in London. She was a founding member of the New Repertory Company, an off-off Broadway group that performed in a former funeral parlor. She then attended Cornell Law School and, for fifteen years, was a legal services attorney in upstate New York. She now lives in Manhattan.